TRADITIONAL IRISH
FLUTE SOLOS
the turoe stone collection

by Vincent Broderick

Music Transcription • Tony Smith
Illustrations • Michael McCullogh
Cover Design • Temple of Design
Cover Photo • Niall McDougald

Order No. wm1190
ISBN No. 1 85720 061 6

Exclusive Distributors:
Walton Manufacturing Co. Ltd.
Unit 6A, Rosemount Park Drive, Rosemount Business Park,
Ballycoolin Road, Blanchardstown, Dublin 15, Ireland

Walton Music Inc.,
P.O. Box 874, New York, NY 10009, U.S.A.

Printed in Ireland by ColourBooks Ltd.

3 5 7 9 0 8 6 4 2

VINCENT BRODERICK   THE TUROE STONE

With the ever growing popularity of his numerous compositions, Vincent Broderick's name and fame are assured in the annals of Irish traditional music. But, of course, that fame has been established long before this decade. His reputation for great round-the-clock sessions of music, with his late and fondly remembered brother Peter, with John Joe Gardiner and Kathleen Harrington or with fellow musicians from East Galway or the Pipers' Club, - was country-wide even before Robbie McMahon penned his epic account of 'The (1956) Fleadh down in Ennis' -

> They came down from Dublin so hearty and gay
> They brought Leo Rowsome to show them the way
> Himself and Seán Seery they played all day
> With their flute-player Vincent Broderick

I have known Vincent Broderick since the late '50's, that's more than 30 years now. Down the years at the Pipers' Club or at the Fleadhs, wherever I met him, as well as his music, I always especially enjoyed his many stories and anecdotes about musicians and characters of byegone days. Of the many stories I could tell, the one I choose is one that I tell against myself: I had been on a recording trip up North in 1973 and, amongst many other tunes, brought back 2 fine reels played by a Northern flute-payer. They were good tunes for the flute and soon I was playing them regularly at sessions around Dublin. When I played them as 'two Fermanagh reels' in the Pipers's Club one night I guessed from the big grin on Vincent's face that I had 'put my foot in it'. 'The rainbow's End' and 'The Crock of Gold' he said jovially before giving me time and place for their composition. 'You aren't the first one to play my own tunes for me,' he assured me 'But I'd like that they'd get the names right - and the story too,' he added 'there's a story to every tune, you know.'

My many other recollections of Vincent Broderick, musician, raconteur, include the considerable part he played on Comhaltas productions through the '70's and '80's. He took part in several CCÉ Tours, visiting the USA, Canada and Britain, and I also recall the major role he played in several Cumann na bPíobairí shows. In particular I recall the hilarious scenes from the Mummers play in 'Fonntraí' when Vincent played 'Sir Patrick' in opposition to Seán MacTorlach's 'Cromwell'. This involved dialogue, both scripted and spontaneous, sword-fighting, step-dancing in traditional style, etc. You had to be very good or MacTorlach would steal the show, but Vincent could match him for acting or for innovation and took it all in his stride. He would lilt or sing, dance a step, or play the bodhrán and did all these spontaneously if the occasion demanded. I would dearly love to see that Mummer's play again.
Fad Saoil chugat Vincent, and thank you for those great tunes and those happy memories.

Séamus MacMathúna

CONTENTS

Vincent Broderick-The Turoe Stone 4
Coachman's Whip, The................8
Flagstone of Memories, The................9
Tinker's Daughter, The................6
Midsummer's Night................6
Halley's Comet 7
Orion Belt, The................7
Horan's Airport................7
Stone Mason, The................8
Hunter's Moon, The................8
Last Train from Loughrea, The................9
Seven Springs................9
Millennium Reel, The................10
Anna Livia................10
Piper from Ballina, The................10
Lighthouse in the Bog, The................11
Dragon Fly, The................12
Honey Bee, The................12
Lynch's Castle................13
Around the Fairy Fort................14
New Broom,The................14
Whistler at the Wake, The................15
Old Flail, The................15
Lumberjack, The................16
Goat's Path, The................16
Stoney Brennan................17
Salmon Weir Bridge, The................17
Pope in the Park, The................28
Cockstep in the Dunghill................18
Loughrea, The................19
Enchanted Lake, The................19
Wind through the Rafters, The................20
Tattie Hookers, The................20
Pucha's Bush, The................21
Spider's Web, The................21

Bus to Mullahoran, The................22
Old Schoolhouse, The................22
Cregg Castle................23
Four Wind's, The................23
Song of the Birds, The................24
Plasterer's Dream, The................25
Turoe Stone, The................25
Pearse's March to the GPO................26
Seven Noble men................26
Old Grandfather Clock,The................26
Aishling O'Neill................27
Bullaun Slide, The................27
Rainbow's End, The................28
Crock of Gold, The................28
Hellfire Club, The................29
Fox on the Prowl, The................29
Haunted House, The................30
Banshee's Wail, The................30
Mountain Ash, The................30
Spanish Arch, The................31
Midnight Owl, The................31
Rookery, The................32
Woman in the Glen, The................32
Lonely Hills of Aughrim, The................33
Milky Way, The................34
Night of the Big Wind, The................34
Ring around the Moon, The................35
Old Wooden Bridge, The................35
Old Station House, The................36
White Stone,The................36
Down the Rushy Glen................37
Pigeon House,The................37
Carramore, The................38
Ballyarra, The................38
Discography................39
Bibliography................39

VINCENT BRODERICK   THE TUROE STONE

VINCENT BRODERICK was born in Carramore, Bullaun, Loughrea, Co. Galway in 1920. One of seven children, both himself and his brother, Peter were to become interested in traditional Irish music at an early age, mainly due to the influence of their mother Ann. By their early twenties, Vincent and Peter, were to become accomplished traditional musicians and were to follow the example set for them by the musicians of the Ballinakill and Aughrim slopes Ceilí Bands.

In the early 1950's, Vincent, like many others, left the west of Ireland and came to work in Dublin. He immediately joined the Piper's Club in Thomas Street and was to become a regular attender and prominent member. At this venue, Vincent joined with some of the greats of Irish music; Leo Rowsome, Mrs. Harrington, John Joe Gardiner, Willie Clancy, Seán Seery and many more, delighting onlookers with their enthusiasm for Irish music. By the mid 50's, Vincent Broderick's name was to become synonymous with accomplished flute playing and was to be heard on many recordings. Vincent went on to become the All-Ireland Champion and Oireachtas winner only to be followed a couple of years later by his brother, Peter.

As a traditional player, Vincent was associated with the Kincora Ceilí Band and was to become a founder member of the Eamonn Ceannt Ceilí Band with Vi Preston. A very modest man by nature, Vincent was to travel throughout Ireland, Great Britain and America with Comhaltas Ceoltóirí Éireann depicting the best in traditional flute playing with his unique style and breath control, being two of his envied attributes as a player.

Over the recent years, Vincent has spent much of his time teaching flute and tin whistle to people of all ages as well as compiling many of the tunes he has composed over the years. He has also directed, produced and participated in a number of scoraíocht productions, some of which have become All-Ireland winners.

The Coachman's Whip

Reel

The Flagstone of Memories

Reel

The Tinker's Daughter

Reel

Midsummer's Night

Reel

Played by musicians all over the country, "The Tinkers Daughter" was performed and recorded by James Last and his Orchestra. It is more commonly known as "Broderick's

6

Halley's Comet

Reel

The Orion Belt

Reel

Horan's Airport

Reel

7

The Stone Mason Jig

The Hunter's Moon Jig

8

The Last Train From Loughrea   Jig

The Seven Springs   Jig

9

The Millenium Reel

Reel

Anna Livia

Reel

The Piper from Ballina

Reel

The Lighthouse in the Bog

Air

The Dragon Fly

Slip Jig

The Honey Bee

Slip Jig

Lynch's Castle is situated in Galway City and is a monument to one of the town's most grisley legends. In 1493, the Mayor, James Lynch Fitz-Stephan is reported to have hung his own son for the murdering of a visiting Spaniard out of jealously.

Lynch's Castle   Hornpipe

Around the Fairy Fort

Barn Dance

The New Broom

Barn Dance

The Whistler at the Wake

Jig

The Old Flail

Jig

The Lumberjack

Reel

The Goat's Path

Reel

This is a tune Vincent composed to Stoney Brennan who was hung during the penal times for stealing a turnip. There is a monument erected in his honour, in Loughrea, Co. Galway.

Stoney Brennan

Reel

The Salmon Weir Bridge

Reel

The Pope in the Park

Reel

The Cockstep in the Dunghill

Reel

The "Cockstep in the Dunghill" is associated with the 6th of January. It was on this date that old people said the day was a cockstep longer.

The Loughrea   Polka

The Enchanted Lake   Polka

19

The Wind through the Rafters

Hornpipe

The Tattie Hokers

Hornpipe

The Pucha's Bush

Jig

The Spider's Web

Jig

The Bus to Mullahoran

Reel

The Old Schoolhouse

Reel

Cregg Castle Reel

The Four Winds Reel

The Song of the Birds

Air

24

The Plasterer's Dream

The Turoe Stone is a well - known landmark situated in Turoe, a couple of miles from Loughrea in Galway. A huge stone dating to the first century, a cast of which can be seen in the National Museum.

The Turoe Stone

Jig

Pearse's March to the G.P.O.

March

Seven Noble Men

March

The Old Grandfather Clock

Hornpipe

Aisling O' Neill

Planxty

The Bullaun Slide

Slide

27

The Rainbow's End

Reel

The Crock of Gold

Reel

28

The Hellfire Club

Reel

The Fox on the Prowl

Reel

The Haunted House

Jig

The Banshee's Wail

Jig

The Mountain Ash

Jig

The Spanish Arch

Hornpipe

The Midnight Owl

Hornpipe

The Rookery

Reel

The Old Woman in the Glen

Reel

The Lonely Hills of Aughrim

Air

The Milky Way

Vincent, accompanied by his family and Tony Smith, rehearse for his Album ' The Turoe Stone ' at COMHALTAS Headquarters in Dublin.

The Night of the Big Wind

The Ring around the Moon

Reel

The Old Wooden Bridge

Reel

Vincent, at the memorial to his brother, Peter Broderick, in Loughrea, Co. Galway.

The Old Station House

Jig

The White Stone

Jig

Down the Rushy Glen Polka

The Pigeon House Polka

The Carramore   Polka

The Ballyarra   Polka

38

ACKNOWLEDGMENTS.

Tony Smith, without whom this book wouldn't have been
possible and for the long hours he spent transcribing all the music.
Michael McCullogh for all the illustrations
Séamus MacMathúna

DISCOGRAPHY.

'Na Ceiríní '78'	Gael-Linn CEF675
'Eamonn Ceannt Ceilí Band	Avoca Records 33 AV-119
Eamonn Ceannt Ceilí Band	Outlet Records SOLP 1025
'The Mountain Top"	Comhaltas CL14
'The Turoe Stone'	Comhaltas

BIBLIOGRAPHY.

Irish Tin Whistle Legends, Waltons, Dublin.